# THE BRIGHTEST STAR

## BY NOEL KAUFMAN

---

## Reading Skills for Life

### Level A

### Book 3

**AGS®**

American Guidance Service , Inc.
Circle Pines, Minnesota 55014-1796
1-800-328-2560

Development and editorial services provided by Straight Line Editorial
Development, Inc.

Illustrations: Wendy Cantor

ISBN 0-7854-2651-5

Product Number 91705

A 0 9 8 7 6 5 4 3 2 1

# Contents

# 1. Slam Dunk

It all came down to 15 ticks of the clock. Fifteen ticks to make them into champs or chumps. Antonio "Tony" Lopez, star big man of the Garfield Bulldogs basketball team, turned his gaze from the time to the score: 56 to 55. The Bulldogs were down by one with just 15 ticks left. The Crenshaw Cougars had the ball, and the Bulldogs had just used their last time-out.

Coach Sharp was telling the Bulldogs how to keep the Cougars from scoring. "Tony, I want you in the lane to block any shot they take inside. Mario and Jason, you keep close to number 23 and number 10. Juan and Andre, look to swipe a pass. When we get the ball, move it up court fast! Take the best shot you can. Don't forget, we only need two points to win."

The Bulldogs broke out of the time-out, and Tony went to the top of the paint. He turned and looked up into the stands. The Lopez clan was there—his mom, his dad, and his five sisters. They were all on their feet yelling. Marta, Tony's girlfriend, was right next to his mother. She looked small inside his big letterman's jacket. Most of Tony's friends seemed to be there too. They were all on their feet, clapping and cheering: "GO BULLDOGS! GO BULLDOGS!"

The buzzer sounded. This was it—crunch time. Tony's team was just two points away from being the champs of all of Los Angeles. It had not been like this his first three years of high school. Not even close. But Tony had added six big inches over the summer. Now, at 6'8", he was the main man.

With Tony making the plays in the paint, the Bulldogs had beaten team after team—23 wins in all. They had lost only two times. One loss had been to these same Cougars. Now was the time for the champs to rise to the top.

The Cougars came out and set up on the court. Calbert Denton, their big man, was standing right next to Tony at the top of the paint.

Number 10 had the ball and tossed it in to 23. He went left with the ball. 14 . . . 13 . . . 12 . . . Now Calbert moved his bulk through the paint like a bulldozer. Number 23 faked a shot, but Mario did not jump. 11 . . . 10 . . . 9 . . . Now 23 tossed the ball to Calbert, who was going to the hoop. The big dude lifted the ball up for the slam. . . .

But Tony was faster—much faster. He jumped high and batted the ball back the other way. 8 . . . 7 . . . 6 . . . Mario grabbed the ball and was off to

6

the races. So was Tony. Two Cougars got back to try to block the path. 5 . . . 4 . . . Time seemed to move at a snail's pace. Mario faked right and lobbed a high pass to Tony. 3 . . . 2 . . . Tony jumped high, snatched the pass with one hand, and jammed the ball down in the hoop. The buzzer went off. The game ended: Bulldogs 57, Cougars 56. The Bulldogs were L.A. city champs!

Bulldog fans mobbed the court. All of Tony's teammates jumped on him. Then they all fell in a heap. When Tony got back on his feet, Coach Sharp gave him a hug. "You are the man, Tony!"

Then Tony's mom and dad were on the court. He gave them each a big hug. "I knew you could do it," said his mother. She said this in Spanish, too. His dad's big smile said it all.

Right then Tony thought, "Where's Marta?" He scanned the mob on the court, but did not see her. He looked back into the stands. He still could not find her. Where she had been sitting, Tony saw a man dressed in a nice coat. He was looking right at Tony. He held up his index finger and then pointed at Tony. He seemed to be saying, "You are number one." The man winked and smiled.

Just then, Tony felt a tug. He turned to see Marta. He gave her a big hug, lifting her high off the court. "Not bad, eh, Guapa?" Tony said.

"Not bad," Marta said, and grabbed his hand.

The next thing Tony knew, many lights flashed around him. Lots of people were taking his picture. Then a woman from a TV sports show asked Tony how he felt. He did not know what to say. He was so happy. He held up one finger and said, "All I know is, we are number one."

Tony went to shake hands with the Cougars. He patted Calbert Denton on the back. "Good game." He could see that Calbert was feeling down. "Maybe next time," Tony said with a kind smile. Then he went back with his teammates.

After a bit, the mob was taken off the court and the Bulldogs were named champs. Tony's team got a big, gleaming cup that read "2002 Champs—Los Angeles." Tony held it high over everyone. Many lights flashed again.

At last, Tony and his teammates went to the locker room to change. Many people came in and patted Tony on the back. "Great job!" they said. Or "You are the best!" Or "Way to go!"

Tony came out to get on the bus back to school. He saw Marta waiting for him with his sisters. He got a hug from each of them. The last one was Rita. He was two years older than she. They had always been good pals.

"Big T, I am so happy for you. You are a star." Rita always called Tony "Big T" because he was older than she was and also because he was so tall. Tony's smile got bigger and bigger.

A little later, Marta and some of the other kids from Garfield High got on the team bus for the trip back to school. The ride went by in a flash.

Then it was just Tony and Marta. They walked to Marta's house hand in hand. Marta asked Tony if he had seen a man next to her in the stands. At first, Tony said he had not. Then he thought about the man with the nice coat.

"That's Rufo," said Marta. "He's a friend of a friend of Alfredo's. He says he thinks you could play in the NBA. He says he knows a big-time NBA deal maker. The deal maker knows all about you. He says you are the best, and he wants to talk to you about your plans." Alfredo was Marta's twin.

"No way!" said Tony. "He thinks I am the best?" Marta nodded. Tony grabbed her tightly in his arms. "Man, what a night," he said.

When they got to Marta's house, Tony gave her a good-night kiss. Then he went home. On the way, he thought over and over again about the end of the game. "Man, that was so cool!" he said. Then he stopped. He thought about the man in the sharp coat. "What if I can play in the NBA?"

# 2. Rising Star

**T**ony didn't wake up until late the next morning. That was OK because it was Sunday. When he did get up, he could smell something good. His mother had made him a big plate of eggs with chopped meat and homemade salsa. As soon as he sat down to eat, Tony's dad handed him the sports pages from the *Los Angeles Times*. On the front page was a picture of Tony slamming home the last basket of the game. In big letters at the top of the page it said, "Bulldogs Are City Champs." Under that it said, "Lopez Makes Big Plays as Time Runs Out."

Tony just about fell out of his chair. Then he read the story. It told about the game. It started by telling about Tony's block and slam. It said he scored 20 points and made four blocks. It said he was named MVP for all of Los Angeles.

Just then there was a call from Coach Sharp. "Tony, did you see the *L.A. Times* yet? Like I told you, you are the man! You are the biggest thing to come out of Garfield High in a long time. You're just about as big as Jaime Escalante! Just about as big as Los Lobos!"

"I don't know about that, Coach," said Tony. "A math teacher who helped many students do well and a rock band that people know all over the globe are bigger than the star of one basketball game. But thanks just the same. Thanks a lot. I'll see you Monday at school."

"OK, Tony, see you then."

After their meal, Tony and his mom, dad, and sisters went to mass. There and on the way home, they met many people who had read the story about Tony and the Bulldogs. Everyone was glad for him, and glad for Garfield High.

The rest of the day was filled with visits and calls from friends and kin. Most had been at the game or had read the *L.A. Times* story. Tony floated through the day as if walking on air.

At dinner that night, Tony's dad said, "Tony, now you have made a big splash. Everyone knows you. You need to think more about what school you want to go to next year. All those applications you filled out will help. But now the coaches at the big schools are going to want you to play on their teams. You may get a free ride all the way. You're going to be the first Lopez to go past high school."

"But, Papa . . ."

"Antonio, hear what I have to say. Your mother and I could not even get to the end of high

11

school. We had to work to help our kin back then. We still work a lot, so you and your sisters don't have to stop school. Now you have made it. You can go on to a great school—UCLA or Kansas or Notre Dame or St. John's in New York. I don't want you to mess up."

"Yes, Papa."

"And speaking of work," said his dad, "don't let all this fame get the best of you. You need to study so you can end high school on the right note. No big school will let you come if you don't get through high school first."

"Carlos, you can stop now," said Tony's mom to his dad. "I think he knows what you're saying."

After they had cleaned up from the meal, Tony and Rita sat out on the front steps.

"I know Papa wants me to go to UCLA or some other big-time school," said Tony. "I don't want to mess up. I just wish schoolwork was as easy as hoops."

"Don't worry, Big T. You'll do OK," said Rita. "And if you don't, I'll do it for you. I may not know how to slam-dunk a basketball, but I do know how to study."

"You are such a joker!" said Tony, lightly whacking his sister with part of the *Times*. "Thanks for making me feel better."

"Not at all, Big T, not at all."

The next day at school seemed just like Sunday to Tony. Everyone who came up to him at school said something nice. He was getting treated like the Big Man at school. Some of the first-year kids asked him to write his name on their bags and their shirts.

In class, even his teachers said nice things to him. His math teacher, Mr. Ybarra, said, "Nice game, Tony." Even with that, Mr. Ybarra gave the class a surprise math test. Tony had a hard time doing the work. He just could not stop daydreaming about the game.

After class, Tony spotted Marta in the parking lot with some of her friends. Also, there was a man Tony did not know. "Hi, Guapa," he said to Marta. "What's up with you?"

"Tony, you know that friend of a friend I was telling you about? This is Rufo," she said, nodding at the man. He pointed his index finger at the sky and then at Tony. It was the same move from after Saturday's game.

"Uh huh. Hi," said Tony.

"You played a great game this weekend, my man," said Rufo. He reached out to grab Tony's hand. "I don't know if Marta said anything, but I know this big-time NBA dude. He would like to meet with you. He can help you out, man. He can help you get some big cash—for you and everyone at home."

"That sounds good to me," said Tony. They made a plan to meet later. "I have to go work out with my team now. Our next game is just as big as that last one. If we win, we take the next step to being state champs."

On the school court, Tony and his teammates did some sprints. Then they ran some plays. But they also did a lot of joking and kidding. Time and time again, Coach Sharp had to tell them not to goof off: "Not on the court. Not in class."

"But Coach . . ." said Mario.

"Hard work is what got us here," said Coach Sharp. "And hard work is how we will get to be state champs."

After the workout ended, Coach Sharp asked Tony to come see him. When Tony got to Coach Sharp's room, the coach had him shut the door and sit down.

"Tony, have you thought any more about what school you would like to go to next year?" said Coach Sharp.

"Well . . ."

"Here's the thing, Tony. After what you did on Saturday, I've been called by five or six coaches

14

from big schools. They all say they want you to come. Some say they could give you a free ride, Tony. A free ride!"

Tony explained to Coach Sharp that he had gotten letters from many different schools. A few schools' coaches had called him. "I'm still thinking about it, Coach," said Tony. But he added that he did not know where to go.

"If you ever need to talk about this, I'm here for you, Tony. And don't forget, don't go talking to any sports deal makers. Look out for those dudes. They could make it so you couldn't play for any school. The NCAA would take the ball out of your hands."

Tony nodded, but he did not say a thing. Coach Sharp had always been there for Tony, with talk that made sense and smart tips. He had helped Tony know what to do when he got into a fight with his dad or with Marta. Tony wanted to tell Coach Sharp about Rufo and the deal maker. But he also thought about his mom, dad, and sisters. He wanted to help. Making big cash in the NBA would help big time. So he said nothing.

At the end of the week, Tony met Rufo again after school. This time Rufo drove up in a nice new car with the top down. He took Tony for a ride to a very big house in the hills looking down on Los Angeles. There he gave Tony over to Mr. Jake Jensen, the big-time NBA deal maker.

"So this is Antonio Marcos Lopez," said Mr. Jensen. "Star big man of Garfield High, 6'8", 25 points, and five blocked shots a game. MVP of all Los Angeles. I know a lot about your game, Tony. I'm glad to get to meet you."

Mr. Jensen asked Tony to come in. Rufo stayed out with the car. The house was like a dream: a big swimming pool in the back. TV sets that came out of the walls. Even a basketball court inside! And so many rooms. Tony and his mom, dad, and sisters could live there and never find each other. This house had it all.

After taking Tony through the house, Mr. Jensen had him sit in a chair by the pool. "So Tony, I've talked to some NBA teams about you. They think you could play in the big time right now!"

"Me? They want me, Mr. Jensen? I'm just a kid. No way," said Tony.

"Yes, you, Tony." Mr. Jensen nodded. "And I know how tight cash is at your home. I can get you a deal so that you can take care of your mom, dad, and sisters—for a long time to come."

Mr. Jensen said that all Tony would have to do is write his name on the line saying he would let Mr. Jensen help him. He gave Tony the paper and a pen.

"This sounds great, Mr. Jensen. It does seem like the right thing to do," said Tony. "But I just need some time to think about it."

"OK, Tony. Take some time. But not too much time. The NBA draft is in June. If I am going to help you, you need to tell me in May that you are going to play."

# 3. Too Cool for School

**T**ony couldn't help it. He liked what Mr. Jensen had said about making big cash. And he liked the look of Mr. Jensen's house and his cars. Still, he thought about how much his mom and dad wanted him to go to a big school.

"You're going to be the first Lopez to go past high school." His dad's words filled his thoughts. But maybe his dad would see why going to the NBA could be a good thing. Then he and Mama would not have to work so hard all the time. Still, Tony did not know what to do.

Two weeks after their big win over the Cougars, the Garfield High Bulldogs faced the Fremont High Pathfinders. Again, Tony played well. He scored 32 points and blocked six shots. But the team could not stop the Pathfinders. In the end, the Bulldogs lost by five points.

No more games for the Bulldogs. No state champ cup for the school. It was all over. Tony was very upset about the loss. "We could have been the winners," he said to his teammates after the game. "We just didn't play well."

"You may be right, Tony," said Coach Sharp. "But I'm happy that you tried as hard as you did. We had a good run. That Fremont team is good. I don't think anyone will beat them."

On the bus ride home, Coach Sharp sat next to Tony. He said that the coaches of more schools had called him. People from those schools had come to see Tony play. They would still want him to come to their schools.

Later that night at home, Tony was still not happy. "Maybe I should have taken more shots," he said to his dad. "Mario and Andre had a bad night. I needed to take over."

"Don't be so upset," said his dad. "You gave it your best shot. And I still think that the big schools want you to come. I saw some top coaches in the stands at the game."

"Coach Sharp said something about them," said Tony. "So what? Maybe I don't want to go to a big school. Or any school, after Garfield."

Everyone stopped and looked at Tony. "Did you ever think about what I want to do?" he said. "Maybe I want to go right to the big time!"

Tony's dad got very mad. "What are you saying? You haven't been talking to any NBA dudes, have you? You know that could keep you out of school for good, don't you?"

"I don't want to talk about it," said Tony.

"Don't mess it up, Antonio," said his dad. "This is your shot at a big-time school. Your mother and I did not even get through high school. Don't mess it up."

"Right, Papa. I know this story. But it's your story, not mine. Get off my case!" yelled Tony. Then he got up and walked out of the house.

Rita looked at her mother. Then she ran after Tony. She could see him walking far down the street. She ran to catch up with him.

"You know, Papa just wants what's best for you," she said. "He's only trying to help."

"He needs to back off and let me be a man. I am a man, you know," said Tony.

"He just wants your life to be better than the one he and Mama have had," said Rita.

"Maybe I know a different way of making my life better," Tony said. "And I don't need to go to school to do it."

Rita's eyes got big. "You mean you may not go to school?"

"I may not even stay in high school!" said Tony. With that, he started to run. Tony was so tall and fast that soon he was out of sight. "Don't do it, Big T," Rita said to no one. "Don't give it up." Then she turned and went back home.

# 4. No More Math

**F**or weeks after the big fight, Tony and his dad did not say much to each other. Life at home was not good. Tony's mother and Rita tried to patch things up between the two men of the house, but it didn't work.

At school, Tony did not hang out with his teammates much. He tried not to see Coach Sharp. The only one he spent any time with was Marta. She could tell that Tony was not doing well.

"Why are you so mad, Tony?" she asked one day. "What's going on?"

"Not you, too, Marta," said Tony. "I don't want any questions. I don't want anyone telling me what to do anymore. I am a man, you know."

"No one said you aren't," said Marta, taking his hand. "I know you're in a bad way. I just want to help if I can."

Tony didn't know what to say. He wanted Marta's help. But how could she . . . "Marta, can you help me find Rufo?" he asked.

"Yes, Tony. But why?" she said.

"If you want to help me, don't ask questions," he said.

"OK, Tony, OK. We'll do this your way," she said.

Tony met with Rufo the next day after school. They went right to Mr. Jensen's house.

"Tony, it's good to see you again," said Mr. Jensen. "Have you thought any more about what we talked about last time?"

"I have, Mr. Jensen," said Tony. "That's why I'm here. Do you still think I can get an NBA deal?"

"No question. Just say the word and I can do it," said Mr. Jensen with a smile.

"My mom and dad want me to get past high school. So can we wait until after it's over?" asked Tony.

"Here's the deal, Tony, my boy. The cutoff date for saying you will go into the NBA draft is in two weeks. No ifs, ands, or buts. That's before school ends. But what's the big deal? You can say you want to go into the draft and still get the high school thing wrapped up."

"What about going to USC or another school after that?" asked Tony.

"Good question. And one you should think about a lot. When you have been in the draft, you can no longer play NCAA ball. You could still go to one of the schools if you want to. But with your grades and without playing ball . . . I don't think any school will pay your way. What I'm trying to say is, if you want to go to the NBA, doing the school thing isn't needed. In fact, you'll be making so much cash—who needs school?"

"But what about my mom and dad?" asked Tony.

"Look, Tony, I'm your friend, right? I want to help you. You seem like a bright kid. Let me say this as clear as I can: You can help your mom and dad more by jumping to the NBA and getting the big cash now. Who knows what school will be like? More classes. More tests. But no cash. See what I mean?" Mr. Jensen looked at Tony.

"Yes, I think so," said Tony, "but I still need time to think it over."

"OK, Tony. But don't miss the cutoff date. It's the week after next. Miss that and your chances are over," said Mr. Jensen.

"Thanks, Mr. Jensen. I will not forget," said Tony.

That night before falling asleep, Tony thought about what Mr. Jensen had said. "NCAA ball. More classes. More tests. Or NBA ball and big cash."

He turned it all over and over again. "No more classes. No more tests. Plus, big-time cash . . . With cash, I can help my mom and dad. Maybe I can help Rita pay her way to a good school, and the others as well. Mama and Papa would be happy then. Wouldn't they? Papa just doesn't see how the cash is a good thing. No, a great thing. I'll show him. I'll show all of them."

The next day at school Tony had changed. No one could see it at first. But little by little it showed that he didn't care about school anymore. Mr. Ybarra was the first to say something to Tony. It came on the day Mr. Ybarra handed back a math test.

"Mr. Lopez, I see you haven't been doing your work lately. Or did you just forget what we have been studying all year?" he asked.

Tony said nothing as he stuffed the test in his bag. He had gotten a D. So what?

"If you do not start to do better work, Mr. Lopez, you may not pass this class," said Mr. Ybarra. "And if you do not pass this class . . . Well, you may be back here again next year. OK, Mr. Lopez?"

"That's what you think," thought Tony, but his lips did not move.

At lunchtime, Tony was sitting alone on a bench. Rita came up to him and sat down. "What's up, Big T?" said Rita.

"I just got a D on my math test, Rita," said Tony.

"Don't fret, Big T. The way I see it, when you make it in the NBA, you will not need much math . . . just what it takes to keep tabs on a lot of cash," Rita said.

Tony looked very surprised. "What do you know about me and the NBA?"

"Marta let slip that you had met Rufo and another man," said Rita. "A dude who can get you into the NBA."

"Marta!" Now Tony was mad. "What other things did she tell you?"

"Nothing. But the way I see it, if you go to the NBA, I also don't have to study."

"What?" Tony couldn't make sense of what Rita was saying. She was always at the top of her class. Rita liked school! Tony looked like he was going to yell at her. Then, through gritted teeth, he said, "Rita, stop thinking that right now! You're smart! You get good grades! You can get out of high school and make it at a big school!"

Just then, Tony's counselor, Ms. Shaw, came by. "Tony, I need to see you right away."

Tony nodded. He turned to finish talking to Rita. But by then the bell had sounded. She got up to go back to class.

"We'll work on this at home," said Tony, but his sister was off to her next class.

# 5. Don't Give Up

**T**ony watched Rita walk away. After a little bit, everyone had gone to class. Tony rose from the bench to go see Ms. Shaw.

Tony was not happy about this at all. Why should he have to meet with anyone? What was so bad about a low mark or two? Was it a crime to take one or two nights off from school work? Tony kicked a trash can, but then he felt bad when the clunk rang all over.

As he waited to be asked in by Ms. Shaw, Tony found he was thinking about old times. Ms. Shaw had been on his side from his first days at high school. She had been there with a kind word or with hints about the right path to take. But she didn't just tell Tony what to do. She let him make the calls. He liked her for that.

There was that day in that first year when one of the kids in the top class had called Tony an ugly name. Tony didn't want to look bad in front of his friends. So he said that he would fight the other kid after school.

Ms. Shaw had passed by just then. She asked Tony to come see her after his next class. Even today, more than three years later, Tony remembers each thing they had said in that meeting:

"You know the school rules about fighting, don't you?"

"Yes, ma'am."

"You don't want to get kicked out of school, do you?"

"No, ma'am."

"Tony, you've been at Garfield for a short time. But I can see that you're a bright kid. Too bright to get mixed up in a fight with some dude who calls you a name. Am I right?"

"I . . . Yes, ma'am."

"Good. I'm glad we had this little chat. I'm also glad to see that you know how to turn the other cheek when kids talk trash. That's going to help you go far. Trust me. Now get to class."

"Yes, ma'am. And thanks."

What would Ms. Shaw have to say this time? Tony was not feeling much like a star standing in front of Ms. Shaw's room. He made a small sound with his throat.

"Come on in, Tony. Pull up a chair," said Ms. Shaw.

Tony sat down next to her desk. "Uh, you wanted to see me?" he asked.

"Tony, I'm going to get right to the point," said Ms. Shaw, peeking over the top of her glasses. "I think you have been slacking off in classes—not doing homework, not studying for tests."

"Did Mr. Ybarra . . ."

"You don't need to know how I know—just that I know," said Ms. Shaw. "Now, what's going on?"

Tony did not say a word. He looked down at his hands.

"Look, Tony. I know you're sad that basketball is over. Maybe it didn't end like you wanted it to. But life goes on. High school goes on. And you have classes to pass so you can go on. I know you can do the work. And so do you."

Tony shifted in his seat.

"Have you thought more about the school you would like to go to next year?" asked Ms. Shaw. "You know they all will want you to get through high school, don't you?"

"Uh, yes, ma'am. I think so," said Tony with words that sounded very small.

"Well, if you have any questions about it, come see me. OK?" said Ms. Shaw.

"Yes, ma'am," said Tony.

After talking to Ms. Shaw, Tony walked home alone. He had a lot of thinking to do. He dropped his bag, picked up his ball, and went to a court at a park just one block from his house.

The court was all busted up. It had weeds shooting up through the cracks. Some were up to Tony's waist. But it was the place where Tony had first played hoops. It was also where he liked to come to think.

First, Tony shot from the stripe. Then he shot from the left side, then the right side. Each shot swished through the hoop. The more he shot, the more he thought.

What am I going to do? he thought. (Swish.) Mom and Dad want me to stay in school. (Swish.) That means more studying and more tests. (Swish.) Maybe I can get a pays-for-all ride to a big school and play NCAA hoops. (Swish.) But Mr. Jensen thinks I can make it in the NBA now. (Swish.) That would mean big cash for me and for my mom and dad. (Swish.) I could help them work less. (Swish.) Who knows what will go down if I pass on the NBA and go off to school? (Swish.) I may not get a shot at the big time later on. (Swish.)

"Tony! Tony!" The sound of Marta calling pulled Tony from his thoughts.

"Huh?" he said, and for the first time in 12 shots the ball clanged off the rim. "Oh, Marta, I didn't see you."

"Tony! Look! I did it!" said Marta, holding up some pages. "I got into Harvard! The letter came today! They want me to come, and they will give me cash to help pay my way!"

"That's great," said Tony. But his feelings did not go with his words. He felt as if his life was about to end. Harvard. Number one school. No way could he get into Harvard. "Besides," thought Tony, "they don't have a very good basketball team there."

Tony had been thinking about his NBA deal so much that he had not tuned in to Marta's plans. "How could she go away without me?" he thought. "I need her."

"What's wrong, Tony?" asked Marta. "You don't seem like yourself. Are you sick?"

Now Tony was feeling mad again. But he held it in check for Marta. "Must have been my lunch. Look, Marta, it's great that you got into a good school. I'm very happy for you. But I have to go home now and take care of some things. I'll call you."

He gave her a kiss on the cheek and ran off. "But Tony . . ."

Too late. He was out of sight.

# 6. The Big Play

**W**hen Tony got home, he found three letters from different schools. UCLA, Kansas, and Arizona were all asking him to come and play. Three big-time schools, all with NCAA banners to show off. Tony added these letters to the pile he had on his desk. Nineteen schools had said they would like him to come. He had even visited some of them.

His trip to UNLV in Las Vegas was the first time Tony had been outside of Los Angeles. He had liked the coaches and kids he had met. Still, school was school. It was the NBA that was the big time.

That night after eating, Tony went to study. But his thoughts were not on his books. First, he thought about his mom and dad. Then he thought about Rita. Then Ms. Shaw. And then Marta. They were all messing up his plans! Couldn't they just let him be? Still, deep inside, Tony had to admit that these people were not the real problem.

"Tony, Marta's on the line for you," called Mama.

When Tony picked up the line, Marta sounded mad. "Tony, you said you would call me. It's after ten. I have to go to sleep."

"Forgive me, Marta. I have a lot going on," said Tony.

"What's up with you?" snapped Marta.

"I don't want you to go to Harvard, Marta," said Tony. "Stay with me. When I make it in the NBA, I'll get us a house."

"What are you talking about, Tony?" said Marta. "The NBA is years away for you. Besides, just because I go away to school doesn't mean we have to stop seeing each other."

"With you in Boston, and me who knows where?" said Tony. He was just about yelling.

"We can see each other at Thanksgiving or Christmas. And we can talk most days," said Marta. "Maybe you could even go to a school on the East Coast."

"Don't tell me what to do," said Tony. He hung up without one more word.

"What's up, Big T?" said Rita. She had just wrapped up her homework.

"I can't talk right now," said Tony. "I've got to go meet some friends."

With that, he grabbed his coat and left the house. At first, Tony didn't know where he was going. But the more he walked, the more he could see what he needed to do. "It's time for me to be a man," he thought. "I need to do what is right for me."

He reached into his coat pocket and got out a small card—it was from Mr. Jensen. Tony called him right away.

"Mr. Jensen. It's Tony Lopez. Forgive me for calling so late. I need to talk to you," said Tony.

"I'm here when you need me, Tony," said Mr. Jensen. "Where are you?"

"I'm outside Garfield," said Tony.

"Sit tight. I'll be by to pick you up right away," said Mr. Jensen.

Not long after that, Tony was sitting next to Mr. Jensen in a fast, sleek sports car.

"So, Tony. What did you need to see me about at this time of night? Do you need some cash?" asked Mr. Jensen.

"No, not that. I just needed to tell you about my plans," said Tony.

"OK. You do that," said Mr. Jensen.

"Marta, that's my girlfriend. She found out today that she got into Harvard, and they're going to pay for her to go," said Tony.

"Good for her," said Mr. Jensen.

"The thing is, I was thinking we would be with each other next year. She's my best friend. She helps me out when I'm down. She helps me know what to do, what path to take. But now she's going away. So I know I have to get on with things and go with what's right for me. Do you know what I mean?" said Tony.

"You bet, Tony," said Mr. Jensen.

"The way I see it, I may not even get out of high school at this point. Math and stuff, you know. So why not go for the NBA? You said teams want me. You said now is the time. You said I could make it to the big time. Didn't you?" said Tony.

"Yes, I did. But we have to take this one step at a time," said Mr. Jensen with a friendly look on his face. "First, you need to take me on as your one and only deal maker. After that, we can talk about the NBA, the cash, the house, the car—all that stuff. But before that, I want you to see what you're getting into."

They drove for a bit without talking. Then Mr. Jensen's car pulled into the lot of the Staples Center. That's where the Los Angeles Lakers play basketball. They went inside a back way. They came out into a vast space with many, many seats. The big area for the seats was dark, but the court was lit up.

"Go on, Tony. Give it a try," said Mr. Jensen. He handed Tony a ball and gave him a push.

Tony went down to the court. He ran to one end and slammed the ball through the hoop. He went to the other end and hit a three-point shot. Then he went to the mid-court line. He looked up. Mr. Jensen came walking down.

"What do you think?" asked Mr. Jensen.

"This is the best," said Tony.

"There may be a home for you here, Tony," said Mr. Jensen. "But you have to go through the draft."

"Just tell me where to write my name," said Tony. "This is a move I want to make."

Tony rode back with Mr. Jensen to his hillside home. There, Tony wrote his name on two forms. One said he would work only with Mr. Jensen. The other said he was putting his name on the list for the NBA draft.

Then Mr. Jensen drove Tony home. "Some teams will want to see you play before the draft," said Mr. Jensen. "There is a tryout next week. I can get you in. If you shine there, you can make it."

"Sounds good to me," said Tony.

It was long after midnight when Tony got back to his house. All of the lights were out. Tony went up to his bed. His math pages were sitting on his desk. Tony picked them up and looked at them. Then he dropped them in the trash can.

# 7. Down and Out

**T**he next day, Tony went to school without telling his mom or dad about his plan with Mr. Jensen. He drifted through his classes with his thoughts far from school. He wanted to get out on the court and work out so he would be in top shape for the tryout. That was the big thing now—the tryout. Show up big there and the NBA teams would fight over him.

"Mr. Lopez. Mr. Lopez! Can you answer the question?" Mr. Ybarra's words pushed him out of his dream.

"Uh, uh. What was the question again?" asked Tony.

"Just forget it, Mr. Lopez," said Mr. Ybarra with a sigh. "But you should stop this daydreaming and get to work. Our last test is coming up. And you know how much you need to do well on it. You need at least a B to pass this class!"

Tony was saved by the bell. He went out to have lunch. Again, Rita found him sitting alone on a bench.

"Big T, where did you go last night?" she asked. "Did you and Marta have a fight?"

"I just needed some time to think," said Tony. "Marta and I will work things out. Besides, I think I have a plan that will make everyone smile."

"What's that, Big T?" asked Rita.

"Not now, Rita," said Tony. "You'll know it all when the time is right."

Rita looked at him for a long time. She had more questions than he had answers.

"OK, Big T. We'll do this your way. Just don't mess up, OK?" said Rita.

"Don't you mess up, Rita," said Tony. "You're going to stay in school, no ifs, ands, or buts. You know what I'm saying."

"Give it a rest, Big T. Like I have to do what you tell me to," she said.

Tony got mad: "Rita!" But she turned away from him and went off with her friends.

Tony didn't run into Marta all day. He went outside after school hoping to see her. But she didn't show up. So Tony went to the court to work out a little with his teammates.

The next day after school was when the fireworks hit. Mr. Jensen had talked on a sports radio show about Tony. The facts got to the

*Los Angeles Times* and there was Tony again on page one of the sports: Garfield Star to Jump to NBA.

Tony's mother was very upset when she read this. She went at him as soon as he stepped into the house. "How could you do this, Tony?" she said. "How could you throw it all away, after all we had hoped for you? And you didn't even tell us!"

Tony's dad hit the roof. "No kid of mine is going to mess up a shot at going to a big school. Call that Mr. Jensen right now!" he yelled.

"No, Papa. This was my idea. I want to go to the NBA. I'll make it big. Then you and Mama will not have to work so much," said Tony. "I thought a lot about this. I'm not made for more school. It's just too much work for me. Basketball is my thing. I can do it. I will do it."

"Not in this house," said Tony's dad. "If you don't get out of the deal you made with Mr. Jensen, if you don't do it today, you take your things and get out of this house!" Then he said some things in Spanish that made Tony know this was the way it would be.

"Fine!" That was all Tony said to his dad. He grabbed a big bag. He stuffed it full of some of his things—some shirts, some shorts, his ball. He came back and kissed Rita, all the other girls, and his mom. Then he left.

Tony marched down the street to school. After a bit, his pace dropped. Then he stopped. "Where am I going to go now?" he thought. "Marta's mad at me. My dad just tossed me out of the house."

Then he thought of Mr. Jensen. Again, he pulled the card from his coat pocket. But when he called, he got the tape: "This is Jake Jensen. I'm not here right now. After the beep, leave your name, number, and the time of your call. I will get back to you just as soon as I can." BEEEEP!

"Mr. Jensen. It's me, Tony. I need help. My dad tossed me out of the house after he read the *L.A. Times*. He wants me to back out of our deal. I said no to that. So now I don't have a place to stay. I will call back later," said Tony.

Then Tony went to the court at school and shot around. He ran into Coach Sharp there.

"Tony, I saw today's *L.A. Times*. I thought we had talked about this," said Coach Sharp. "Why didn't you come talk to me first, before going this way? No big school is going to want you now, Tony."

"But Coach, I had to do what was best for my mom and dad and Rita and the others . . . and what's best for me," said Tony.

"Your mom and dad asked you to do this?" asked Coach Sharp.

"No. They didn't want me to do it. But they don't know what's best. They don't see how my getting into the NBA will help them," said Tony.

"Maybe you're right," said Coach Sharp. "But I think going to school is best for someone with your smarts. Anyway, now you'll have to watch your back, Tony, and your pocket, too. Lots of dudes are going to want to be your friends. But what they want more than that is the cash you'll have."

"OK, Coach. I'll watch out," said Tony.

After Coach Sharp left, Tony's teammates showed up at the court. They all slapped him on the back.

"Way to go, Tony. You're going to the big time now," said Mario.

"Don't forget your friends when you're on the top," said Andre.

The boys shot some hoops. Then they went home. Not Tony, though. He had no home to go to. But when he got outside, there was Mr. Jensen in a brand-new sports car that was different from the one he had been driving the other day. "Hop in, Tony," he said.

They sped down the 10 to the coast. Before long they were in Santa Monica. Mr. Jensen took Tony to a house that looked out on the sea. Inside Tony met an old NBA player—Bill Goodyear. Mr. Jensen had worked with him some years back.

"Jake tells me you have the stuff to make it in the NBA," said Bill Goodyear. He had played point for the Lakers for many years. One year he had been an All Star. "Well, I can tell you that Jake will treat you right."

Tony wanted to talk to the old star but found that he couldn't say much. After a bit, Bill Goodyear got up and left. Then it was just Tony and Mr. Jensen.

"Man, Mr. Jensen. You know Bill Goodyear!" said Tony.

"I know him and many other NBA greats," said Mr. Jensen. "Now why don't you call me Jake?"

"OK, Mr. Jen . . . I mean Jake," said Tony.

"You can crash here for a bit," said Mr. Jensen. "This is a place I rent for when my players are in Los Angeles. There is food. And if you give a call, I will have someone come and take you to where you need to go. I've got to run. We'll talk more about the tryout in a bit. OK?"

Then it was just Tony in the house over the beach, looking out at the Pacific.

"Bill Goodyear, man," thought Tony. "I should have had him write his name on my bag or my shirt or something. My dad thought he was the best. And this house, right on the beach . . . The rent here must be out of sight. I'll get a place like this after I make my deal. Then Mom and Dad will see that I'm right. And Marta too. Maybe I can talk her out of Harvard when she sees this."

Tony did not sleep well that night. When he woke up the next day, he wasn't as glad to be there all alone. He called Mr. Jensen's house. Someone there said he would come and take Tony to school. Tony got there just after the first class of the day had ended. As he walked to his next class, he saw Marta—for the first time after their fight.

"Marta, uh, how have you been?" said Tony.

"I've been OK, Tony. But I've been missing you," she said. They hugged and kissed. "Meet me after school, OK? I have someone I want you to meet."

"I'll be there," said Tony.

Going back to school turned out to not be such a good idea. It seemed that all Tony's teachers and all his classmates had read about him in the *L.A. Times.*

Many of his classmates were glad for him. Some wanted to be his new friends. Some just wanted him to go away.

Some teachers were not so nice too.

"Now I know why you have been goofing off so much, Mr. Lopez," said Mr. Ybarra. "You could have saved me a lot of work by just not showing up at all."

When Ms. Shaw ran into Tony, she looked at him sadly. "You could have made it to a good school, Tony. Are you sure you're not messing up?"

At last, the school day came to an end. Tony met Marta outside by the lot. She led him to a bus, the one to the city of Bellflower. They got off there, and Tony followed Marta down the street. They walked past block after block of small homes. At last, at the end of one street Marta walked up a path to a green house and knocked. A man in his 30s came out and gave her a hug. Marta waved for Tony to go in.

"Tony, this is my Uncle Jesse. Jesse Ortega," said Marta. "Uncle Jesse, this is Tony."

"Nice to meet you, Tony," said Uncle Jesse.

"Nice to meet you, too," said Tony.

They went inside and all sat down on some old, beat-up chairs. Tony did not know why he was there. He looked at Marta with a question on his face. She got right to the point.

"Uncle Jesse played baseball at Garfield High in the late 70s," she said. "He was the star pitcher. He pitched two no-hitters. He was also very good in school. Only As and Bs all the time, isn't that right, Uncle Jesse?"

"Well, yes," he said. "But I didn't make it to the end. I went to play big-time baseball after only three years of high school. I got a contract right then and there."

"What then?" asked Tony.

"Well, I played a year on an AA ball club. I did well, winning most of my games. See, I could bring some real heat. But then I hurt my arm at the end of the year. They tried to fix it, but it was not the same. I lost my fastball at the age of 18," said Uncle Jesse.

"That's how old I am," Tony thought. Then he said, "What did you do then?"

"I tried to make it to the bigs—for five years. But my arm didn't come back," said Uncle Jesse. "So I went back and got my GED. Now I work over in Burbank at a place where they make films. I let cars in and out of a gate all day long. I've been there for 15 years now. The pay is OK, though I wish I made more. Looking back, I wish I had stayed in school. You know, USC and Cal State Los Angeles said I could go there and play baseball after high school. But I thought I could skip the stepping stone and go right to the top."

After their visit with Uncle Jesse, Tony and Marta walked back to the bus stop. They didn't talk much.

"What did you think of Uncle Jesse?" said Marta.

"He's cool. Just had some bad luck," said Tony.

After the bus dropped them off at school, Marta said, "Well, I have to go study for a big test. See you around."

"We'll talk, right?" said Tony.

"OK," said Marta as she walked away.

Tony called Mr. Jensen. The same dude who gave him a lift to school picked Tony up to take him to the house by the beach.

That night, Tony kept thinking about Uncle Jesse. "He seemed like a good man. He just had bad luck, that's all. That will not happen to me. Besides, Mr. Jensen will look out for me. And I will make it in the NBA. I just know I will."

Then Tony thought about Marta. "She still thinks I'm messing up. How can I make her see that this is what's right for me? She's going to the East Coast anyway. Why should I be taking time to deal with what she thinks?"

Tony told himself he was right, but he still felt bad inside. He felt like he was deep under the sea and couldn't get to the top for air.

He went outside on the deck to get some fresh air. He could see the light of a lighthouse down the coast a way. It flicked on and off, on and off. Tony wished Marta was there to see how good life could be. "Maybe then she would know why I'm doing what I'm doing," he thought.

When Tony went back inside, he saw the *L.A. Times* from the day before. He found the sports page and read the story about him and the NBA draft. It was nice to see his name on the page, just like it had been before. But now, he didn't know how to feel about what the story said.

"I don't have to go to school again," he said to no one. Then, without knowing why, Tony thought about the math test Mr. Ybarra would be giving the next day. "He doesn't think I can do the work," thought Tony. "I could ace that test. I know I could. When I put my mind to math, I can do it. I'll show him. Then I'll walk out of Garfield for good."

# 8. Tryout

**O**n Tuesday, Tony drove back to school with one of Mr. Jensen's friends. When Tony walked into the math class, no one was more surprised than Mr. Ybarra.

"You showed up, Mr. Lopez," he said. "Did you forget that today is the last test?"

"No way, Mr. Ybarra," said Tony through gritted teeth. He walked over to his desk and sat down. "Bring it on."

Mr. Ybarra passed out the test and the kids got to work. Tony looked over the pages. The questions looked like ones he had seen before. "I can do this," he thought. And he got to work.

Tony finished the test with time left on the clock. He read through his answers one more time. Then he walked to Mr. Ybarra's desk, dropped the pages on top, turned, and walked out without saying one word.

At lunchtime he saw Rita and Marta walking side by side. They came up to him.

"Hi, girls," said Tony. "Nice day, isn't it?"

"What are you doing here, Big T? I thought you dropped out," said Rita.

"And miss all the fun?" said Tony. "No way."

"Wasn't your last math test today?" asked Marta. "Did you go?"

"Uh huh," said Tony. "I couldn't let Mr. Ybarra flunk me."

"So are you going to try to finish high school after all?" said Marta.

"Well, I'm here now. That's all I can tell you," said Tony.

Marta gave Tony a hug. So did Rita.

"How are Mom and Dad?" asked Tony.

"Mom is very upset. She doesn't know what to do," said Rita. "Dad's upset, too. He just has a different way of showing it. He's digging a lot outside the house. He says he wants to put in a bunch of new plants."

"Dad's putting in plants?" said Tony. "Man, what did I do?"

"You should call them," said Rita.

"No way. Remember, HE tossed ME out of the house," said Tony. "I think he has to make the first move."

"But Tony . . ." said Marta.

"Can't we talk without you telling me what to do?" said Tony. He was talking to Rita and Marta.

"Look, I'm out of here. I have to stay in shape for my NBA tryout."

He gave Rita a hug and kissed Marta. Then he left. Mr. Jensen's friend came to pick him up and take him to a court where he could work out. He did some skill drills. He made some shots. Then he played in some pickup games with other dudes at the court. He smoked them all, but they weren't very good.

The rest of the week, Tony was in and out of school. He showed up for the last test in each of his classes. He tried not to talk to anyone— anyone but Rita or Marta. Then after school, he was off to work out again.

On Wednesday of the following week, kids at school got their grades. Tony got an A on his last test in math, so he got a B- for the class. He also got Bs and one C in his other classes. He couldn't keep from smiling. He would finish high school with his class!

"Cool running, Big T!" said Rita, when he told her.

"Tell Mom and Dad for me, OK?" said Tony.

"Can do," said Rita. "Does this mean you are going to try to get into UCLA or Cal State?"

"The NBA, Rita," said Tony. "The NBA will be my school."

"I just hope you don't flunk, Big T," said Rita.

Later that day, Tony met up with Marta.

"Thursday is the big tryout, Guapa," said Tony. "Will you wish me luck?"

"Tony, you know I always want you to do well. I'm glad you finished high school. I still think you need to think about going on to study more. You could do so much, Tony. Don't sell yourself short," said Marta.

"I know what you want, Marta," said Tony. "This is just something I need to do."

That night at the beach house, Tony tossed and turned in bed. The next day would be the biggest of his life. He had to do well and show his skills to the coaches and others from NBA teams who would be on hand. Tony tried not to think about Marta or about his mom, dad, and Rita. But pictures of them kept popping up in his dreams.

At 7:00 the next morning, a ringing sound made Tony leap out of bed. Mr. Jensen was calling.

"Rise and shine, Tony. Rise and shine," said Mr. Jensen. "Today's the big day, Champ. We don't want to be late."

Tony got dressed in stuff Mr. Jensen had left him. It was all brand new. Then he ate a good meal.

He had just finished when Mr. Jensen pulled up. "Let's rock and roll," he said.

"OK, Jake," said Tony.

"That's my boy," said Mr. Jensen.

They drove for a bit until they got to the site of the tryout. Inside Tony met with the coaches and the other players who would take part in the tryout. Calbert Denton was there. So were some of the other top kids Tony had played before. A bunch of kids Tony did not know were there, too. All of them looked like they could play.

The boys were called out onto the court.

"OK, men. First, we are going to do some drills so you can show us your stuff. Then we'll split you into two teams to play a game or two," said the man in charge.

One by one, the boys were asked to show different skills. They ran. They jumped. They shot from different parts of the court. Tony did OK. He was not at his best, but he thought he was doing about as well as most of the other boys.

The NBA reps were all writing notes on pads. Tony tried not to look at them, but he couldn't help peeking over one or two times.

Then the boys were split into two teams— Team Red and Team White. Tony was on Team Red. They played a timed game with refs.

The NBA reps kept on watching and writing.

Tony was not in at first, but after a time-out he was called onto the court. Right away he was banging in the paint with Calbert Denton, who was on Team White.

After two or three trips up and down the court, the ball went to Calbert. He took a shot. Tony jumped to block it, but missed. The ball hit the rim and popped up. Tony and Calbert jumped to grab it at the same time. Tony grabbed the ball first, but they bumped into each other.

When they came down, Calbert landed in an odd way. There was a popping sound. He fell to the court and grabbed his knee. Play was stopped as Calbert rolled around. He was in a lot of pain.

Trainers rushed onto the court to look at Calbert. After a bit, he was taken off to the side. It looked like he had torn something in his knee. His day—maybe his only shot at the NBA—was over.

Tony felt sick. He had just been playing, trying to get the ball. And now Calbert was out. Tony tried to block these thoughts out as he kept playing. Again he played OK, but not as well as he knew he could.

One kid on his team, a boy from Fremont, was lighting it up. He hit shot after shot, made a block or two, and had a one-handed, windmill slam. He put on a show for the NBA reps. In the end, Team Red won.

After the game, Tony talked with Mr. Jensen.

"Well, Tony. You did OK out there," said Mr. Jensen.

"It wasn't my best," said Tony sadly. "I just messed up."

"Don't get too worked up about it," said Mr. Jensen. "I think the reps still like your size and speed. You could still go high in the draft."

"What about Calbert?" asked Tony.

"Who?" said Mr. Jensen. "Oh, that kid who messed up his knee? Too bad about him. But in some ways that's good for you. At least he's not going to be in your way come draft day."

"What do you mean?" asked Tony, sounding a little mad now.

"Look, Tony. This is not a high school game anymore. This is a dog-eat-dog game," said Mr. Jensen. "That kid, what's-his-name, is just one more big man who could have pushed you down in the draft. That's cash out of your pocket."

"And YOURS," said Tony. He sounded very mad now.

"No need to get so upset," said Mr. Jensen. "I'm just giving you the facts, man to man."

"Right," said Tony. "Look, I have to go see Marta."

"OK. I need to go talk to some of the NBA reps. Here's cash for a cab back home," said Mr. Jensen.

Tony pushed Mr. Jensen's hand back. "That's OK. I have some cash," said Tony. "See you around."

"I'll let you know what the reps are saying," said Mr. Jensen. "Talk to you later."

As Tony looked for a cab, he thought about how Mr. Jensen had acted at the tryout. "He wasn't upset at all about Calbert. He said it was good for me. This dude is strictly in it for the cash. Coach Sharp was right. I need to watch my back, even with Mr. Jensen."

On the cab ride to Marta's house, Tony could not stop thinking about Calbert. "We're all just one little bump away from busting something, from losing our shot at the big time. And then what do we have? Look how things turned out for Uncle Jesse—a parking lot job! That is just plain sad. Maybe Marta was right. Maybe my dad was right. Oh, man, what am I going to do?"

When Tony got to Marta's house, she was sitting outside on the porch.

"How did it go?" she asked. "Did you show your stuff?"

"It went OK," said Tony. "But this one dude—you know that big kid from Crenshaw, Calbert Denton—he fell and messed up his knee."

"That's too bad," said Marta. "I know you thought he was cool."

"The thing is, that could have been me," said Tony. "Just one bump, one fall—and it could all be over. It's not just a game anymore."

"You sound so sad," said Marta.

"Maybe I am. Marta, I thought I had things all lined up. Now I don't know what to do anymore," said Tony.

They sat without talking for a long time. Then Tony gave Marta a hug. He said he needed to do some thinking and turned to go.

"Do that, Tony," Marta said. "Think—just like you did on the math test. You know a lot more now. Just use your smarts and trust your feelings. You'll get it right." She waved, and he waved back as he shut the gate.

# 9. The Brightest Star

**B**ack at the beach house, Tony played the tape.
There was a call from Mr. Jensen:

"Tony. Jake here. I talked to some of the NBA
teams that were at the tryout. Things are looking
good. You still have a good shot to be a high draft
pick. Maybe not top ten, but top 30. Anyway, just
sit tight for now. I'll let you know if there are
going to be any more tryouts. Some teams may
want to have you in to take a look one-on-one.
No times set yet. I'll call."

It was late, but Tony went for a walk on the
beach. As he walked, he tossed rocks into the
waves. "OK. Marta and the others are right. I've
messed up big time," he thought. "But I have to
work with Mr. Jensen. We have a deal. So going to
school next year is out of the question."

Tony stopped to watch the shore birds running
up and down the beach. Tony wished he could
run free like the birds. But he felt like he was
locked in a box with no way out.

The next day, Friday, was the last day of school.
Thinking about school made Tony feel bad, but

he went anyway. He wanted to see what a last "last day of school" would be like.

Tony met up with Marta after the first class of the day. At the sight of her, all his feelings came rushing out.

"I need help," said Tony. "I don't know what to do. Mr. Jensen says I could make it in the top 30 in the draft. But now I'm not . . . I mean, I don't know if the NBA is the right thing to do. After Calbert messed up his knee . . . That could have been me, you know."

"OK, Tony. OK," said Marta. She grabbed his hand and led him to a bench. "Can you get out of your deal with Mr. Jensen?"

"I don't think so," said Tony.

"You need to know if you can or you can't," said Marta. "I think we need to get outside help right now. Let's go see Ms. Shaw."

"Not Ms. Shaw. She thinks I've messed up big time," said Tony.

"You want to try to do something about this, don't you?" said Marta. "Ms. Shaw will know what to do."

"OK," said Tony. "Let's go."

They found Ms. Shaw at her desk.

"Hi, Marta. Hi, Tony. Hey, great job, Tony. I see that you passed all your classes. You're going to finish on time," said Ms. Shaw.

"Thanks," said Tony. Then he looked down and didn't say one more word.

Marta hit him on the arm.

"Well, uh, Ms. Shaw, I . . . I need some help," said Tony. "I think I messed up by making a deal to go into the NBA draft. I want out, but I don't know how. I don't even know if I can get out."

"OK, Tony, sit down and we'll take this one step at a time," said Ms. Shaw. "You wrote the NBA, right? And you have a man helping you. What's his name again?"

"Mr. Jensen. Jake Jensen," said Tony.

"I think you can get out of the deal with the NBA. The draft hasn't been held yet, has it? OK, so you just need to write to them to let them know you are taking yourself out of the draft," said Ms. Shaw. "As for this Mr. Jensen . . . the deal you made with him may make it hard for you to play in the NCAA."

Tony slumped down in a chair like a rag doll.

"Still, with your GPA and your test scores, I think you should get into an OK school—maybe even a great school," said Ms. Shaw. "And who knows, maybe if we can break your deal with Mr. Jensen, you may get to play ball someday."

Tony sat up a bit. "You think so?" he said.

"I know so," said Ms. Shaw. "First, you need to write the letter to the NBA to get the ball rolling. Maybe your mom and dad can help you."

"But my dad kicked me out of the house weeks ago," said Tony. He was down again.

"Let me see what I can do about that," said Ms. Shaw. "Come see me after school."

"OK, Ms. Shaw. I'll do that," said Tony. "And thanks. Thanks a lot."

"That's what I'm here for, Tony," said Ms. Shaw.

Tony and Marta went to their next classes. Andre gave Tony a high five when he walked into shop class. They talked about his tryout, about the end of school, and about the coming year. But Tony didn't feel like telling anyone about what was going on with him. So much was still up in the air.

At the end of the school day, Tony went back to see Ms. Shaw. His mom and dad were with her!

"Uh, hi, Mom. Hi, Dad," said Tony.

His mother grabbed him and hugged him tightly. "Oh, Tony," was all she could say.

The two Lopez men looked at each other.

"Dad . . ."

"Tony . . ."

They gave each other a great big hug.

"We are filled with pride," said Tony's dad. "Ms. Shaw let us know that you ended school with good marks. We're so happy you'll finish this year with your class. Ms. Shaw also let us know that you want our help to get out of the NBA draft and the deal you made with that Mr. Jensen. We want to help you any way we can."

His mother was nodding.

"I checked around a little for you, Tony," said Ms. Shaw. "The cutoff date for dropping out of the draft is not until a week before the draft. That's at the end of June. So you have time."

"OK. I'll do what I need to," said Tony.

"As for Mr. Jensen . . . I made some calls. Here's what I found out: It may cost you some cash to get out of your deal with him. You'll have to look at what you agreed to. He could make it hard on you. In the end, it's up to you and him to work this out. But if he gets mean, we can get some help to fight him."

"I don't think we'll need that, Ms. Shaw," said Tony. "I just need to talk to him, man to man."

"Is that smart?" asked Tony's dad. "I mean, I bet this dude is very sharp. He's not going to like this one bit."

"Dad, you have to trust me on this. OK?" said Tony.

Tony's mom gave his dad a look. "OK, Tony. We'll do this your way."

That night, Tony did not go with his classmates to the end-of-year school events. His dad lent him the truck, and Tony drove out to the beach house. He had called Mr. Jensen in the afternoon and asked to meet him there.

When Tony got there, Mr. Jensen was on the back deck.

"Hey, Tony! How was the last day of school?" said Mr. Jensen.

"It was OK," said Tony. "You know—lots of high fives and good-byes."

"So what's up?" asked Mr. Jensen.

"Well, first of all, I want to give you back this stuff," said Tony. He handed Mr. Jensen a bag with all the basketball stuff he'd been given. Then he gave him $75.00. "And here is the cash you've spent on me."

"Stop right there, Tony," said Mr. Jensen. "What's this all about?"

"Look, Jake. I mean, Mr. Jensen. I want to thank you for all you have given me," said Tony. "Driving me around, letting me stay here, helping me get a shot in the NBA. It was nice. No, it was great—at least, at times it was. But I've been doing a lot of thinking this past week. The NBA just isn't for me. Not yet, anyway."

"Tony, Tony, Tony," said Mr. Jensen. "Who is telling you that? Is it your mom and dad? Is it your girlfriend—what's her name—Martha? This is your shot at the big time. Do not mess this up, my man."

"No one is telling me what to say," said Tony. "I came to this by myself. I'm not going in the draft. I sent a letter to the NBA today."

"You WHAT?" said Mr. Jensen.

"Look. You can take me to court. You can do what you want. But I've got to back out of our deal. This is not for me."

"Well, if that's the way you feel about it, I can't stop you," said Mr. Jensen. "But it may cost . . ."

"I'll pay it," said Tony. Then he turned and walked away. On the drive home, all Tony could think about was the letters he wanted to write to UCLA and the other schools. He wanted to find out if any of them still wanted him to come play, after he got all this mess sorted out.

Back on the deck, Jake Jensen didn't move for a long time. Then he slapped his hand on the rail, locked up the house, got in his car, and drove off. It was time for him to look for a new "star." This time, he would need to get one who wasn't so bright.